# Rockpeople

# Beyond Chester Creek

*Words, Rockpeople, & Photos
by Joel Carter*

Canukshuk Artworks
Minneapolis, Minnesota
www.rockpeople.org

*Rockpeople: Beyond Chester Creek*

Text, Rockpeople, and Photographs by Joel Carter

Cover and book design by Brian Donahue / bedesign, inc.

12  13  14  15  16    6  5  4  3  2

ISBN: 978-0-9745847-3-7 (hc : alk. paper)
ISBN: 978-0-9745847-2-0 (pb : alk. paper)

Printed in China by Pettit Network, Inc.

For my children — Anouk and Alec,
mi esposa Natalia,

and for all my family, friends, and patients
who have taught and continue to remind me
what is important.

～

My thanks and gratitude to Brian Donahue, Bruce Petitt,
and June Kallestad for their guidance and contributions.

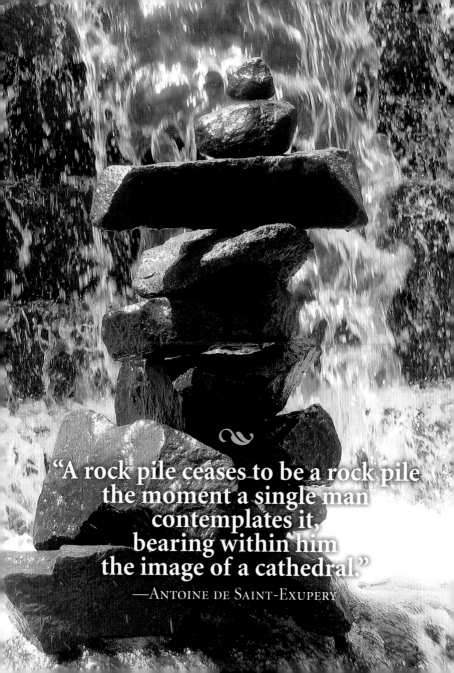

"A rock pile ceases to be a rock pile
the moment a single man
contemplates it,
bearing within him
the image of a cathedral."

—Antoine de Saint-Exupery

# Introduction

The 2003 Rockpeople project was an introspective reflection about the discovery of the healing gifts of creative and artistic processes. On one level not much has changed but from other perspectives everything has changed. Back then it was about a personal 'reckoning' of past and an evolving sense of identity. It was a journey that began with a sweat lodge in Taos, New Mexico, and the rocks on the shores of Lake Superior. It ended with the rocks and stones in Treblinka – the extermination camp in Poland where my grandmother and perhaps my grandfather were victims of the Holocaust. Now it has moved beyond the internal rearrangement of sense-of-self to broader reflections relating to the mystery of the human journey.

Joseph Campbell, the notable Jungian mythologist, once described the mid-life crisis as getting to the top rung of the ladder and realizing it is leaning up against the wrong building. I've learned that climbing back down and starting from scratch takes time and focused intention. It's well worth the effort considering the alternative of staying put in places not intuitively authentic. That said, I realize that on the other side of the great divide between 'then' and 'now' I'm still as perplexed about life's unfolding but a bit more practiced in being present in the moment and grateful for it all.

'Reckoning' suggests the calculation of a ship's position based on the stars. Before charting a new course it's important to know where once we came. I don't think knowing what lies ahead is all that important anymore. What's important is accepting the adventure willingly.

As it goes with insights from my time with the Rockpeople or Inuksuks, so perhaps it goes with the lessons of life;

1) Find the balance point of each chosen part.
2) Find what fits and what doesn't.
3) Don't force things when they don't work.
4) Don't try to recreate what was before.
5) Take the risk of the seemingly impossible possibilities.
6) Know when less is more.
7) Let the process guide the finished product.
8) Be present in the creative moment.
9) Use the broken parts to add stability to the whole.
10) Get out of the way if things begin to collapse.
11) At the end take time to reflect and listen to what the teaching is.
12) Move on to what's next.
13) Be thankful.

The Rockpeople project has evolved in many ways beyond the trails and rocks of my beloved Chester Creek in Duluth, Minnesota, to the earth and stones of Brazil, Uruguay, Chile and New Zealand. I've moved from beyond introspection to external observations, from emergency physician trying to save lives to a palliative physician who cares for the dying, from medicine to healing, healer to artist, lecturer to storyteller, divorced to remarried, flying solo to fatherhood.

Changing to a palliative medicine career has allowed me to see life better. When I see a cloud now, I see a cloud. I see my parents age onward, the trees that once stood on the street I grew up on, the gentleness of how my little daughter tucks her doll in at bedtime the same way I put her to sleep, my little boy running opened armed and broad smiling as I walk in the door. I can see it all now – to the essence of the moment – when before I was too busy and too engaged in 'things' to pay attention to what was important.

An old friend, Steve from Duluth, Minnesota, who I worked with for years in the emergency room would often call and his first line when I picked up the phone was always; "JOEL! What's it all about?" My standard response was "Steve! I don't have a clue." But now I do.

Life can take one well beyond the imaginings of self if we are open to not being attached to how it 'should' turn out. There will always be 'choppy waters' we need to navigate during the early, middle and later years. The rough times are perhaps essential to shake up the idea of what we believe life is about and teach us what our purpose may be.

'Rockpeople — The Chester Creek Inuksuit Anthrology' is gone. A sold out print run of 3,000 with little sustained publicity or promotion for reasons beyond my knowing — one of life's little surprises for me I suppose. My sense is that it connected with those on a similar path of inquiry and members of the Rockpeople Tribe who are drawn to the pull of the natural world to ground oneself.

And now to what is new — *Rockpeople: Beyond Chester Creek*. May the rocks and musings continue to serve a purpose, provide perspective and wisdom for what is important in finding meaningful ways to live out our lives. ⁓

Joel Carter
2012

Sanctuary

# Sacred Moments

I decided to stop
praying and instead consider
my whole life a prayer.

Now all my moments are sacred,
it's more time effective,
and my knees aren't so sore.

Pinnacle

# Cannon-ball

There comes a time
when we have to fall into
the arms of the universe
whether we want to or not.

When that time comes we can
either jump or wait to be pushed.

Jumping seems to be the better option to me.

At least I can cannon-ball and make a bigger splash.

Apprentice

# The Wind

Taking your chances with the wind
means you have to be prepared
for the parts of you that are
blown away,

as well as

those
that
are

uncovered.

June

# Bum Bites

She said, "I wonder if you
take life too seriously?"

I said, "What else is there
to be serious about?"

Then I turned her over
and bit her bum.

Invocation

# Spiritual Practice

After years of questioning and searching
I finally decided what my
spiritual practice is.

It's called life.

It's an all inclusive denomination.
The theology is dynamic, fluid,
and always changing.
The pulpit is everywhere.
The central doctrine is conscious love,
compassion, and awareness.
All contributions are mainstream
random acts of kindness.
And new members are always welcome.

Black Madonna

# Emergence

Life isn't so much
about growing up
and out,
as it is about
emerging within.

Mourning

# Deep Places

I don't think we are suppose to
"recover" from the deep places life takes us.

I think we are called to embrace
the darkness, the unknowing and
the joy of being alive.

Alec and Anouk

# My Moments

When I let go
of my fear
of tomorrow,
and held on
to being present
in all my moments,
I realized
I was happy,
and had
everything
I needed.

Center Stage

# Mainstream

Why would I want to be mainstream?
God forbid that I should ever be mainstream!

.

The Shaman

# Flying

The best part
of letting go
is getting the
chance to see
if you can fly.

# Sailing

May the compass of life be mystery.

May the soul set sail with the thrill of adventure.

May we steer directly into the unknown

with our eyes wide open,

our heart full —

following the breath as it fills our sails.

The Wise One

# It

Some choose to run from it.
Some choose to ignore it.
Some people cover it up.
Some people pretend it doesn't exist.

Some choose to dive into its center,
and in the silence
they change.

The Gatekeepers

# The Soul's Gate

The heart and life's circumstances
eventually lead to the soul's gate.

The journey then is to unlatch the soul and open,
as opposed to jumping over the top
or sneaking underneath.

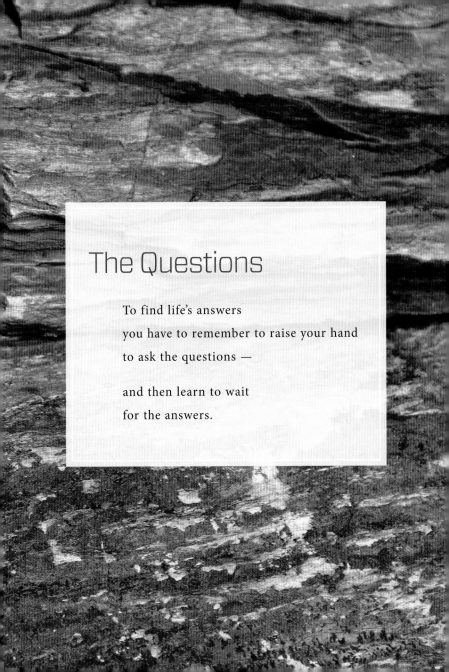

# The Questions

To find life's answers
you have to remember to raise your hand
to ask the questions —

and then learn to wait
for the answers.

Perspective

# Great View

The best part
about having
one's life up in
the air is that
it gives one a
great view of
everything else.

Alignment

# Balance Point

I've been stacking rocks
on the shore of Lake Superior
for the last number of years.
I've found that the rocks have
balance points that you can feel.

I've also found the higher the stack
gets the less control you have —
and you need to let the rocks find
the balance point themselves.

Proud Mother

# Unfolding

It's often said
that the universe
is unfolding
as it should.

So I decided —
I am too.

Jedi

# Instead

God forbid you should
forget to live your life,
and live someone else's
life instead.

# Sojourner

Getting older isn't
so much about being
a frequent flyer, as
it is about being a
seasoned sojourner.

You travel lighter,
learn life is full of accommodations,
your valuables are always with you,
and you come to love the unexpected
twists in the road.

On the Edge

# The Details

I finally gave the details
to the Universe to work out.

It's been around
a lot longer
and probably
knows
what
it's
doing.

The Flame Within

# A Small Flame

I excavated
into the deep.

Sat there
with its
dark silence.

Danced that dance
of grief, pain,
and loss.

And after
sometime in the
vast cavity of my soul,
a small flame ignited.

And I saw you
were already
waiting there,
in the soft
tender chamber
of my heart.

The Embrace

# Dancing

She said she had
a gift for me
so I asked
what it was.

She said it was the gift
of woundedness,
and that it
was given
with love.

Then she smiled at me with
a twinkle in her eye
and began to dance.

And she danced,
and she danced
until she disappeared.
After sometime
I began to understand.

And then I began to dance too.

# Getting Comfortable

After more than a decade

she finally decided

that she would just

be comfortable

with

it.

# Something Solid

Falling into the
abyss is not such
a bad thing.

After plummeting
through the darkness you
eventually hit something solid.

That's when the door
opens and you finally
know you're home.

The Ancestors

## More Room

Today I realized
all the anger and rage
were finally gone.
And there's so
much more room now
for everything else.

Little Buddha

# Changing

It's amazing when you
haven't moved a muscle
or even taken a breath
and you find yourself
in a completely different
place.

# Full Circle

She asked him, "What is it like to sit
across from your son at this point in your life,
not having experienced that for yourself?"

My dad looked at me
and quietly said
with a soft smile,
"It feels good."

And tears welled up in my eyes as I realized
that I was able to be present for my dad in a
way he never received for himself, even as he sat in
the place his father never experienced having
been killed in the Warsaw Ghetto Uprising
when he was a boy.

And in some way the agonizing cross-generational
grief, loss, and pain had finally come full circle
and was healed in a sacred moment of connecting
with my father.
And as our stories merged, the story of his father
merged with him,
And then there was silence,
and I was finally with my dad.

We had both come home together.

Princess Snow Water

# Life's Crucible

I've come to realize that life's crucible is love.

Webster's defines crucible as
"1: a pot of very refractory
material used for melting and
calcining a substance that
requires a high degree of heat
2: a severe test."

I've also come to realize that within love
is the crucible of healing.

Webster's defines heal as
"1a: to make sound or whole."

Perhaps that's what the journey is all about.

The remnant of Treblinka, the extermination camp in Poland where the Nazis murdered 800,000 Jews, the majority from the Warsaw Ghetto. Victims included the author's grandmother and possibly his grandfather (his grandfather may have died in the Warsaw Ghetto Uprising). This photo was taken in autumn, 2000.

# Treblinka

There's nothing left but stones.

My Dad and I dedicated two
of them for his parents.

We stood there for some time
with the gentle breeze.

"I won't be back,"
he said, "but I'm glad I came."

I made a map of
where the two
stones were.

And I knew
some day
I would be
here again.

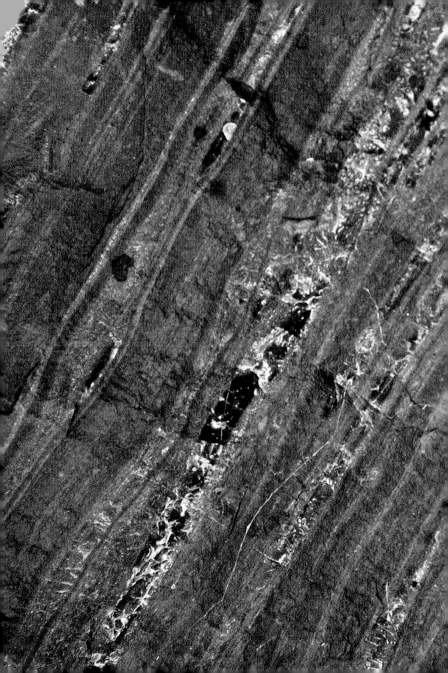

# Silence

Sometimes it's important
not to say or think anything —
in order to let
the silence
speak the
truth.

El Charrua

# Other Side

On the other side of it all –

there is always something new.

Sparrowhawk

# Together

We're all in this thing together.

Alec

# Seeing

When the window shade raised
and he saw the sunlight, the trees,
and the blue skies
his eyes beamed and he smiled with such joy
that you knew he was simply happy to be
a part of it too.

La Brava - Montevideo

# Complicated Gig

I said to her, "You know
this human being thing – it's a complicated gig."

"That's a good line," she replied. "Can I use it?"
"Of course," I replied.

Then she closed her eyes,
smiled — then slowly faded away.

Padre y hija

## Too Much Too

"Papi," she said. "I love you too much."

"That's OK," I whispered,

"because I love you too much too."

The Storytellers

# The Story of Stories

He said finally, "I got a story for you,
Doctor Carter.

But it's not a story of anything in particular.
It's a story of all the stories."

"Those are the very best kind,"
I said as I pulled up my chair.

Western Spirits

# Flowers and Chocolate

"Life changes," I told her.
She nodded, paused, and then replied.
"I just didn't imagine it would be this much
or winter could be so cold."

So I offered her some merino wool underwear
and a thyroid supplement as a bonus anniversary
gift.

Needless to say – it didn't go over very well
so I decided to just stick to flowers and chocolate
after that.

The Dreamer

# The Dare

"Dreams are never in crisis," he dared us to believe.

So we did.

The Threshold

# The Truth

This life force depends on three things;
    Performance Status
        Nutritional Intake
           Strength of will-to-live

So I asked him, "How's your will-to-live
doing today?"

"Not too bad to tell you the truth.

But it'll get a whole lot better
once I'm off this bed-pan."

Abu

# Granddaughter Medicine

"I don't have any better or more potent medicine
than what's curled up beside you,"
I said to him.

He glanced down at his little grand-daughter
at his side – then looked up at me
and we both knew it was true.

Hoping

# So Bright

She had one of the hardest journeys I had seen.

But as it ended she said
"It's so bright!"

and we knew she was going to be OK.

For Eric

# Finished Strong

He didn't have much time left
so when she flew in to visit
he stayed up all night with her
to share stories and watch the sun rise
as any young gentleman would do
given the chance.

Sacred Circle

# Moving On

They had already moved on without her
so there really wasn't too much
holding her back
from moving on herself.

Tranquility Base

# Good Enough

She wasn't scared of dying
because she had loved
everyone the best she could
and thought if that wasn't
good enough
then it wasn't her problem.

Mindful

# Apple Pie

He walked up to me with one of her famous
apple pies as thanks.

He said that it was her favorite recipe.

And that he and the girls were doing the best
they could.

I took the pie home after a few minutes
of remembering knowing I would never be
the same.

New Zealand

# Seeing The World

I tried calling her to see how she was doing
but she never answered
so I decided that she
must have gone out to 'see the world' like her
answering machine had mentioned.

The Otak

# Important Stuff

When he finally could talk again he turned
to his wife
and said with his first words in a long time
"I love you."

Then he asked for the phone to call his boys
and told them the same.

He didn't remember much of anything
but that was OK because he always knew
about the most important stuff.

The Angel

# All She Needed

She said that she wasn't scared
because she had a little angel
that told her she'd be fine
and that was all she needed
not to worry.

Montevideo Brava II

# Sacred Space

Sacred spaces aren't so much
about where you are
as opposed to how you are
with where you're at.

Contentment

# Best Story

I asked her, "Of all the stories you've lived—
what was one of the best?"

"When I met him," she said instantly.

Then everything seemed to change
and she didn't need much of anything else.

Creek Dancers

# Dinner Menu

"Oh my — I didn't think it would come to this," she said.

After a bit of time I asked, "Do you think you want to keep going?"

She paused, smiled, then said—

"It'll all depend on what they're serving for dinner."

The Changeling

# Past Lives

"I think I was here before," I said, "but it seems so long ago.

"Perhaps it was one of those past lives," she said. "Hard to know which one I suppose," I pondered.

Once you come across one of those past lives – it's hard to know what to do with them.

# Sadie Hawkins

There was nothing we could do
except hear how they met
at a Sadie Hawkins Dance 32 years ago
and had loved each other ever since.

# Packer Fans

She could only say a few words being so weak.
I asked how long they had been married.
He said thirty years.

"What's your secret?" I asked.
She said "We liked each other and he's a much
nicer person than I am."

Then he said "We both decided to like each
other."

I said that was very convenient, especially being
that they were both Packer Fans and all.

Trail Blazers

# Trail Head

"Doc – looks like I'm at the end of the trail,"
he said.

"So how was the journey?"
"A lot of bumps and curves along the way
I guess.

I never thought I'd end up here.
But man – what a ride!"

Survivor

# The Hard Part

In most cases I told them that the dying is easy.
The hard part always is saying good-bye.
They both looked at me and then at each other
and it was quiet for a long time after that.

Reunion

# Small Stuff

We hadn't seen each other for years
but the conversation
seemed like it started back up from the day before.
A lot had changed and yet nothing had changed.
But we both agreed there was a
whole lot more 'small stuff' around now
than there was before.

# Legacy

We both wondered what kind of legacy
we would have left after a hundred years
had passed.

Then his little boy tapped on the door window,
smiled, waved, then playfully slammed
the door shut.

We decided that was as good as any answer we
would get.

# Fashion Conscious

Always being the fashion conscious type
she had a burst of energy in the morning
and rallied enough so she could apply
her blue eye shadow for the last time.

Which was not surprising
since her family had said she wouldn't be
caught dead without looking her best.

# Broken Parts

I told them that the most important parts
are the broken ones
because its really what makes
everything else possible.

# Growing

She was ten feet up in the air and just able to pull
herself over the edge when she turned
and looked down at me beaming and said

"See Daddy – I *told* you I could do it!"

And we both grew up a lot in that moment as she
ran off into the distance.

The Wizard Patterner

# The Wizard

I asked him, "what kind of wizard are you?"
He smiled and said, "what makes you think I'm
a wizard?"

I said it was the only thing that made any sense
since I had already seen him in action

and knew what he was capable of.

Elm Street

# Heaven

Heaven is not a place that we go to.

It's a place that we recognize.

—Mayan Tradition

# In the End

I think at the end
to think that one had lived all of it
as best one could
would be important.

To know that it was worth-while.
To have loved well, and to be curious
about what comes next.

Gallery Exhibit, 2010

Sacred Spaces: 10 artists in 30 days
Tychman Shapiro Gallery —
Center for Jewish Arts and
Humanities

Gallery Exhibit, 2011

Living Green Expo
Art as gateway for community
engagement — sustaining nature
and culture
Fine Arts Building/Minnesota State
Fairgrounds

# About the Artist & Author

*J*oel Carter, born in Winnipeg, Canada, is a freelance writer, artist, storyteller and physician. He practiced emergency medicine in Duluth, Minnesota, for over a decade, and in 2002 was awarded a Bush Medical Fellowship by the Archibald Bush Foundation to pursue interests in End of Life Medicine and Physician Leadership. He completed his pain and palliative medicine fellowship at the Dana Farber Cancer Institute — Harvard University in Boston, Massachusetts, and training at the Physician Leadership College — University of St. Thomas in Minneapolis, Minnesota. He currently is medical director of a palliative care program in Minneapolis, Minnesota, where he treats patients and lectures on many topics related to end of life care. His clinical interests include complex pain management strategies as well as the use of storytelling and narrative as they pertain to the psychosocial aspects of dying patients and their families. His short stories have been published in the *Los Angeles Times, Reader's Digest,* and the *Annals of Emergency Medicine.* His creative rock sculptures have been invited to be part of formal exhibitions and can continue to be found along Chester Creek in Duluth from time to time. ∽